Easy as ABC

Zz

Warren Rylands
and Samantha Nugent

LET'S READ AV² BY WEIGL™
ADDED VALUE • AUDIO VISUAL

AV² provides enriched content that supplements and complements this book. Weigl's AV² books strive to create inspired learning and engage young minds in a total learning experience.

Your AV² Media Enhanced books come alive with...

Audio
Listen to sections of the book read aloud.

Video
Watch informative video clips.

Embedded Weblinks
Gain additional information for research.

Try This!
Complete activities and hands-on experiments.

Key Words
Study vocabulary, and complete a matching word activity.

Quizzes
Test your knowledge.

Slide Show
View images and captions, and prepare a presentation.

... and much, much more!

Go to **www.av2books.com**, and enter this book's unique code.

BOOK CODE

Q988552

AV² by Weigl brings you media enhanced books that support active learning.

Published by AV² by Weigl
350 5ᵗʰ Avenue, 59ᵗʰ Floor
New York, NY 10118

Website: www.av2books.com

Library of Congress Control Number: 2015940629

ISBN 978-1-4896-3569-3 (hardcover)
ISBN 978-1-4896-3571-6 (single user eBook)
ISBN 978-1-4896-3572-3 (multi-user eBook)

Printed in the United States of America in Brainerd, Minnesota
1 2 3 4 5 6 7 8 9 0 19 18 17 16 15

052015
WEP050815

Project Coordinator: Katie Gillespie   Art Director: Terry Paulhus

Weigl acknowledges Getty Images and iStock as the primary image suppliers for this title.

CONTENTS

2   AV² Book Code

4   Discovering the Letter Z

6   Starting Words with Z

8   Z Inside a Word

10 Ending Words with Z

12 Learning Z Names

14 The Z Sound

16 Z Sound Words

18 Two in a Row

20 Having Fun with Z

22 Z and the Alphabet

24 Log on to www.av2books.com

Let's explore the letter

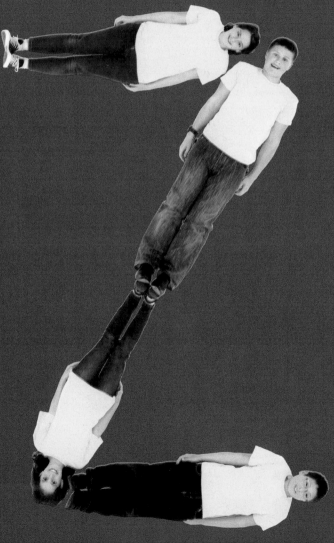

The uppercase letter **Z** looks like this

The lowercase letter **z** looks like this

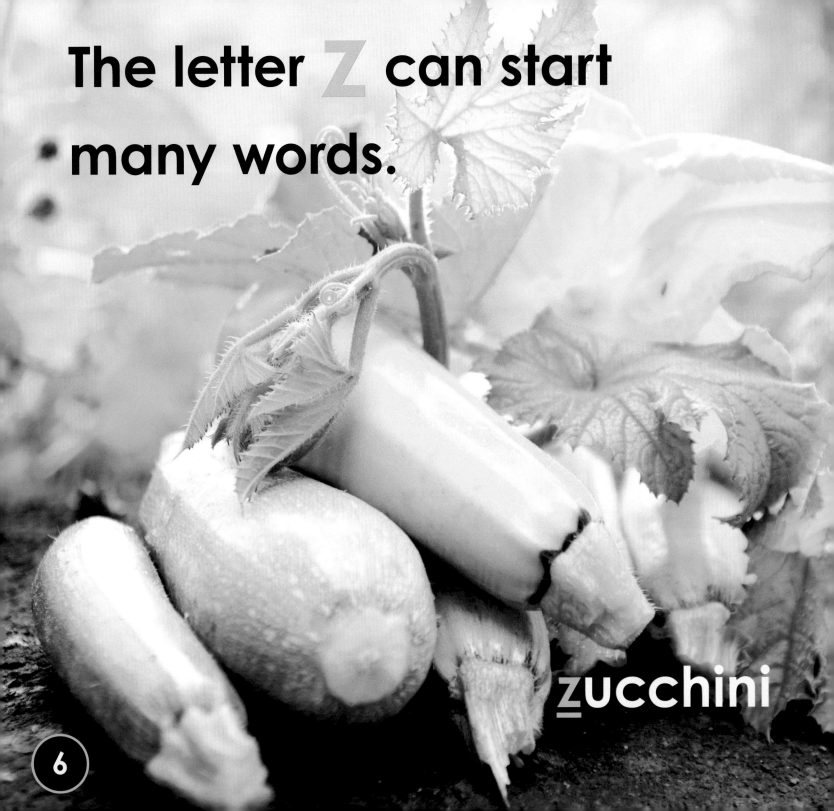

The letter Z can start many words.

zucchini

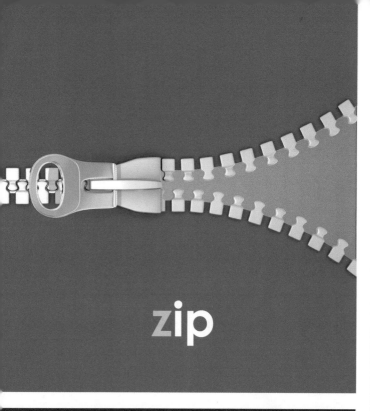

zip

zoom

zero

zoo

7

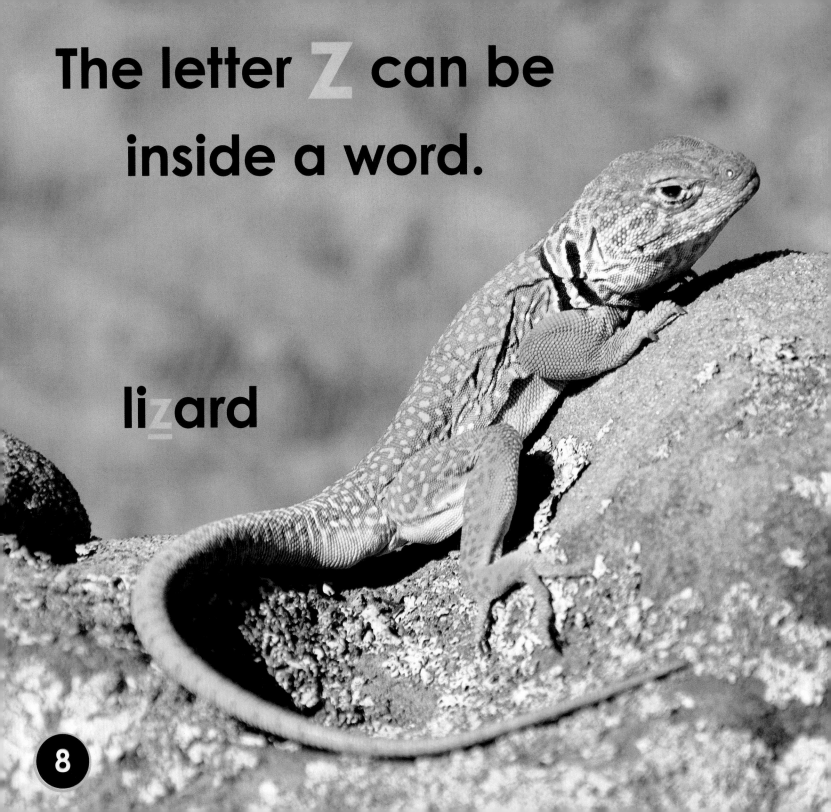

The letter Z can be inside a word.

lizard

blaze

cozy

maze

pizza

9

The letter **Z** can be at the end of a word.

topa**z**

waltz

fizz

quiz

whiz

11

Many names start with an uppercase Z.

Zack

Zamir likes to jump.

Ziggy plays soccer.

Zane can run fast.

Zelda loves flowers.

13

The letter **Z** makes one sound.

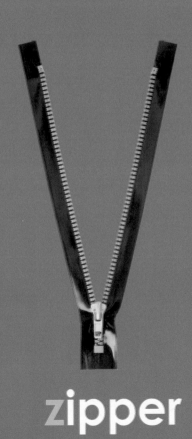

zipper

jazz

The word **zipper** has the z sound.

The word **jazz** has the z sound.

Many words have

the Z sound.

zap

size

dozen

zone

froze

17

When the letter Z comes twice in a row, it makes only one z sound.

buzz

dizzy

puzzle

fuzz

grizzly

Having Fun with Z

Zack likes to zip and zoom.
He will zip until he is dizzy.
He will zoom
until things look fuzzy.

The lazy lizard
does not zip or zoom.
He likes to eat pizza
and listen to jazz.

Being cozy is what
the lazy lizard likes best.
He ignores Zack
when he whizzes by.

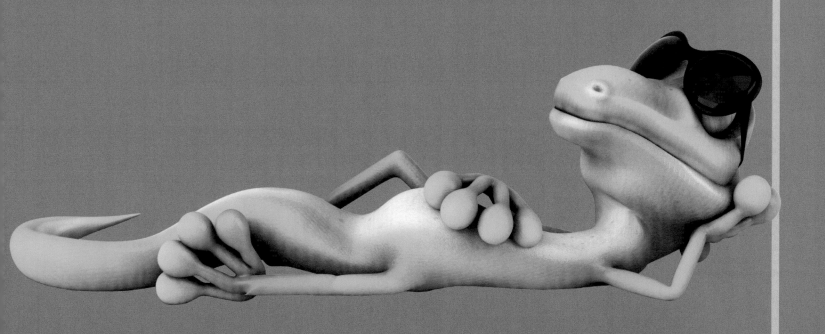

The alphabet
has 26 letters.

Z is the last
letter in the alphabet.

Aa Bb Cc Dd Ee

Ff Gg Hh Ii Jj Kk

Ll Mm Nn Oo Pp

Qq Rr Ss Tt Uu Vv

Ww Xx Yy Zz

Zz